This book is dedicated to my mother; her courage
and inspiration came late in both of our lives but she
never gave up the desire to show me how much she
loves me.

It is easy to share a story of success however, when
we share a story about challenges we have
overcome, it allows others the opportunity to see
their own potential!

BY
NANCY MUELLER

damages. If you have any questions or concerns, the advice of a competent professional should be sought.

Manufactured in the United States of America

ISBN – 13: 978-1514395554
ISBN – 10: 151439555X

Testimonials:

Healing The Child Within is a book you want to read…and you absolutely *have* to read it. Not only will it provide you with insight, understanding and appreciation for the journey Nancy has taken on this adventure called life, it will also give you inspiration, courage and belief that you too, can overcome, conquer and walk through the pain of your past so that your future can be brighter and richer than you ever thought possible.

Dr. Susan Bock
Soulful Coaching

"Healing the child within is truly inspiring and heartfelt. The integral message in this book is that we can choose to heal the past and live the life we so deserve. It is easy to think that we are the only person who is a victim of circumstance, however, there are always two sides to a story. Nancy and her mother bravely share their stories of how they became estranged, but most importantly how they became reunited through Nancy's sheer determination to heal her past and become empowered through teaching valuable tools and techniques she offers within this book. It is a *'must read'* and if you are looking for change, then this book will certainly change your life!"

Michelle M. Wright
Author of REMEMBER *'Everything is Possible'*

HEALING THE CHILD WITHIN, Life Is All About Choices

Nancy Mueller's new book *Healing the Child Within, Life Is All About Choices* shows us the importance of childhood and how it impacts our lives. She helps you understand, accept and move past your unresolved issues and feelings. Use this book as way to heal yourself an others.

Joe Nunziata, author of Karma Buster, Spiritual Selling and many others

Table of Contents

Foreword

Preface

FOREWORD

What Is "**Your Story**" And Why Does It Matter?

Someone once asked me, "When you say that **Life Is All About Choices**, isn't that statement an intense study of the obvious?" My answer is "NO" and this book will show you "WHY" we make the choices we make and "HOW" our choices have created the life we currently live.

This book can change your life; first because you were drawn to the contents of what you have read so far and second by putting into practice the tools and concepts within the book.

My name is Nancy Mueller and I am a Life Sensei (Sensei roughly translated means teacher). When I was in my 30's I became a student, competitor and teacher of the Martial Arts. My coaching business actually started because I wanted to teach Self-Defense to women.

Although my workshops were very popular I soon realized that while women were attending in record numbers, they weren't interested in learning the basics behind the techniques they were being taught. As a Martial Artist, this prompted me to ask myself "WHY do these women keep attending my workshops if they don't want to understand the basics of self-defense?" It was then I realized the philosophies I was teaching them, along with the techniques, was something they were holding on to and incorporating into their lives, their careers and their relationships. This is what kept them coming back, week after week and this is what was helping them to create huge shifts in their lives.

Over the years, I have taught many workshops both LIVE and virtual that covered Fearless Public Speaking, Self-Defense, Creating Your Mission Statement, Money Mindset and many others.

The information being shared with you in this book is based on a common "missing link" that I found to exist and I am really excited to share it with you because, **"I KNOW" that this information is LIFE CHANGING** - if you are open minded enough to think outside of the box and question what you believe.

It's Quite Simple: When you want your life to change, change will happen when you understand how to change your story.

I will be sharing tools and techniques that you can begin applying as soon as you are ready. Whatever your reason for picking up this book, I believe that the information in this book has the power to transform relationships, careers, financial situations and lives.

You simply have to be willing to change your story…

Let's start with my definition of "Your Story"

We all have a story that we believe is the definition of who we are or why we live the life we live today.

Stories such as: "I'm smart, I can do anything I set my mind to, money comes easily to me, I have always been healthy, I make good relationship choices," these stories empower us to live a purposeful life.

But what about people who have stories such as: "Money has always been hard to come by, Growing up I never had the necessary tools that would help me be more prosperous, I don't have the right education, I come from a long line of unhealthy people, Other people always seem to be luckier than me." These negative stories we tell ourselves can be endless and leave us feeling depressed, hopeless or even suicidal.

Our thoughts are based on the stories we tell ourselves, over and over and over again. Our thoughts become our beliefs, our beliefs become our habits and our habits rule our choices. Every choice we make is based on our story that we BELIEVE to be true.

To help you understand this concept I will use a product example. Let's say that you grew up drinking a certain brand of coffee. When you moved out on your own, you continued to buy and consume that same brand of coffee because that is what you know (that is your story about coffee). Then one day you see a commercial for a different brand of coffee. The first several times you see the commercial, the brand of coffee doesn't even register in your mind because your story is about the brand you currently drink. Manufacturers spend billions of dollars in advertising money to try to get consumers to switch from their current brands to the new products and most people have to see or hear a commercial at least eleven times before they will even think about the new brand because our current brand (our story) is so ingrained in our subconscious belief.

Now, this might not seem very important when we are talking about a brand of coffee or what toothpaste you buy, but what about your story concerning your health, your religion, your finances, your relationships, your career, your parenting choices or what you see every time you look in the mirror?

If your story includes a lifestyle that has you feeling a lack of energy, lost, depressed, anxious and even stuck in your current situation or relationships, the tools and techniques in this book can teach you how to "HAVE", "DO" or "BE" anything you desire in your life!

When the student is ready, the teacher will appear.

~ Light On The Path by Mabel Collins

What if life isn't about "becoming" anything?

What if it is about "unbecoming" everything you have become so far?

PREFACE

I was 50 years old when my husband of 32 years told me to file for divorce. I felt as though the bottom had fallen out of my world and my world, as I knew it, came to a standstill. How was I going to move forward, face my children, my friends, or myself? Everything I had known for the last 36 years was rapidly changing and my life was totally out of control. I had always felt a huge sense of accomplishment for being married so long and it was a big part of who I was. I was sad and confused and even though I knew that my marriage was not healthy for either of us, I wanted desperately to hold on to the only security I had managed to build in my life. I wanted him to want our marriage to be better. I wanted to keep my commitment to my marriage. But just as much, I wanted to be free of our toxic relationship, however, I did not know how to free myself from the relationship and stay committed to my marriage at the same time.

I was so tired of living a lie and trying to keep up appearances of a happy marriage. Friends used to tell me that I was so lucky because I had a nice house, beautiful daughters, and from their perception, the ideal marriage.

Their comments reminded me of a quote from Jerry Lewis, *"people can complement you on your new shoes, but only you know how much they hurt your feet!"*

Never be envious of what someone else has because you do not know the price they paid to get it!

It was during this time that I decided to write my first book titled, Chocolate or Vanilla, Life Is All About Choices. It was also during this time when my mother, who had been mostly absent from my life, decided to come back into my life.

I live in California and my mother lives in Ohio and one day she called me to ask me if what she had heard was true, "was I really getting divorced?"

My mother and I really did not have much of a relationship. Prior to her call our relationship consisted mainly of me avoiding her as much as possible and trying to understand how to live with the aftermath of her parenting choices.

Life has a way of forcing you to deal with situations and events when you least expect it as was the case with me when I received that call from my mother. I had just finished writing my first book and I was preparing to publish it but her phone call gave me pause. I now wondered if I really wanted to move forward to publish my book because I was not sure how my mom would handle it. So I decided to have a conversation about it with my mother, "Ma, I want you to know that I wrote a book and I would like to publish it. However, it does not put you and dad in a very favorable light.

Due to the relationship that you and I are trying to build, I would like you to read it and if you ask me not to publish it, I won't."

My mother agreed to read it and I emailed the manuscript to her. Two days later she called and said, "Well, you're right, this book certainly does not put your father and me in a very favorable light but I think you should publish the book." I was a little taken aback so I asked her why she wanted me to move forward with the publication.

This was her answer, "Nancy, I have never been there for you your entire life and I certainly had no idea that you were so brilliant. I have been watching what you do to teach and inspire women and I am so proud of you. I believe that when you share your story, it will help women understand why you do the work you do and your book will give them that information.

Besides, everything you have written is the truth and it is time the truth came out. Please let me be here for you now and see this through with you."

Needless to say, I was speechless. Who was this woman and what had she done with the mother I had known all these years? So, I published my first book and it began to help many women in more ways than I could ever have foreseen. Not only did it help others, but it changed the relationship between my mother and me.

Now, five years later, this book shares what I refer to as The Missing Link. Have you ever wondered what is holding you back from having everything you want in this life? I hear people tell themselves and anyone who will listen that if only they were more educated, had more money, lived in a different neighborhood, could attend the right school, had a better childhood, etc. then their life would be better. The truth is, these are stories they tell themselves.

Every person has a story, some stories bring us closer to our hearts desire and others pull us farther away.

CHAPTER 1

Nancy's Story

Growing up, my two constant companions were fear and anxiety. My fear came from the constant anger that led to abuse from my parents and my anxiety came from trying very hard not to do something that would cause them to take that anger and abuse out on me!

For the first 17 years of my life I was constantly told that I was nothing, that I would always be nothing, that I was lazy and that I was worthless. Having been told that often enough that was the story that constantly played in my head and that was the story I believed to be true...

When I was a freshman in high school, a woman came to our school to talk to us during one of our assemblies. The purpose for her visit was to encourage us to stay away from drugs. She told us about her drug use and how her choices to use drugs landed her in jail. Her message was meant to keep us from making the same mistakes that she did. I was amazed that she was telling us such gruesome, graphic details of a negative part of her life and I realized that she was sharing her story in the hope that we would choose not to make the same choices she did.

I was raised in an Italian household where the number one rule was, "never talk about what goes on inside our house with anyone who doesn't live in our house." We even knew better than to talk about what went on inside our house with each other. Our number one rule was to "just keep quiet."

Imagine my amazement at hearing this woman sharing her story with all of us. Not only had she experienced some horrific moments in her life, but she was also sharing them with our whole school!

Her words and her story had such a profound effect on me and I remember thinking, "I want to do that. I want to stand up in front of people and talk like she is, I want to motivate and inspire people to make better choices by sharing my story."

Right.

Who was I kidding?

My story was very clear in my head: I was nothing, I was lazy, I was worthless and I certainly knew that I was not smart enough to ever do anything like this lady was doing! Besides, if I **EVER** told **ANYONE** about **ANYTHING** that went on in our house, I was pretty sure that I would burn in hell forever because my story included experiences that were never talked about.

To share my story, I would have to tell people about my childhood memories…

Chapter 2

The Initiation

It was 2:00 in the morning and I was standing on the beach, blindfolded and shivering in the night air. I tried to listen to what was going on around me so that I could get some idea of what was going to happen but all I could hear was the sound of the waves crashing very close to where I was standing. I tried to hear sounds coming from my sister or brothers that would let me know that they were ok but, again, all I could hear was the ocean. I wanted to speak, no, I wanted to scream out and yell at him and ask him what was happening; but I knew better. When we were told to do something we did it, with no questions asked because if we didn't, the consequences would always be brutal. My mind was racing and I was trying to figure out how to get out of this predicament. I couldn't figure out why we had been pulled from our warm beds and were now standing at the edge of the ocean in the middle of the night.

I kept going over the entire day in my head and asking myself what I or one of my siblings could have done that had finally pushed him over the edge. With the roar of the ocean in my ears, the only conclusion I could come to was that one or more of us had finally angered him to the point that he had decided to bring us out here in the middle of the night and drown us. I am not sure if I was afraid or looking forward to ending the madness that was my life.

Then I started thinking about the fact that there were five of us and there was no way he could drown all five of us at the same time so I started to devise a plan. I was the oldest and it was up to me to figure a way out of this.

I figured if I grabbed the baby and started running and just kept running until I found help that I could save at least two of us and maybe put an end to this madness.

Finally I heard my mother speak up and tell him that he had to stop because we were too afraid. Even though I could not see his face through my blindfold, I could feel his fury and held my breath to see what would happen next.

I felt him pick me up and throw me in the back of the truck and when all five of us were in the truck together.

I heard the door slam and then the driver and passenger doors slam and the truck started up.

I breathed a sigh of relief because once more we had made it through another one of his initiations. It was 1964; I was 7 years old.

One of the things I never understood was why my mother didn't intervene and protect us from our father's abuse. It wasn't until years later, when I asked her that very question, she told me my father used to tell her if she didn't do exactly as he wanted, he would leave her and she would have to find a way to raise five children by herself. She used to think she was helping us by yelling and screaming at us to keep us in line. She thought that if she could make us "strong" that we would be tough enough to deal with life.

ON THE ROAD AGAIN

My father could never make up his mind where he wanted to live so we constantly moved back and forth from California to Ohio and back again. By the time I started High School, I had attended 13 different schools

FULL HOUSE

Because he was frequently out of work, it meant that we never had any money. Our father's lack of work also meant that we often lived with different relatives. When I was in kindergarten we lived with my father's parents in a 3 bedroom home, which meant that there were 13 people living in their house with only one bathroom.

At Christmas we would watch our cousins get presents wrapped in bright paper with pretty bows. Like most children, my siblings and I believed in Santa Claus and it was difficult for our mother to help us understand why there were no presents under the tree for us.

BEYOND ABUSE

One day my father was mad at my sister and decided to punish her. He tied her to a post in our kitchen, pulled her shirt up to her shoulders, put water on her stomach and then rubbed salt all over her wet stomach. He kept pounding her stomach and rubbing the salt into her skin because he wanted her to admit to something she did wrong. My sister just stood there, tied to the post, staring off in the distance at something only she could see the while he took his anger out on her. I watched her stomach get redder and redder as the skin was rubbed raw from the salt.

It never occurred to me to try to come to her rescue; on the contrary, I was glad it was her and not me.

My happiness that his attention was directed towards my sister instead of me was usually short lived, because sooner or later he would turn his sadistic thoughts to both of us at the same time by making us fight each other.

Fighting each other meant that when the fight was over, one of us was the winner, and one of us was the loser. There was never an option for me to say that I didn't want to fight because that would mean he would find a way to take his anger out on me.

I would much rather take my chances with my sister than with him so I fought her until there was a winner; and I NEVER lost.

To this day, my sister has the scars, both mentally and physically as a result of our forced fights. As a child, trying to survive in my world, victory seemed the most important thing to be proud of. It never occurred to me what harm I might be doing to my sister. I thought that winning a fight meant that I was strong and losing a fight meant that I was weak.

I learned that when you are weak, you get hurt, when you are strong, you get hurt less.

My father never tied me to a pole; instead he seemed to favor beating me with a fiberglass fishing rod. Death was something I found myself praying for quite often during my childhood. I truly felt that I meant nothing to no one, and no one was going to save us.

KARATE

I grew up in the era of Bruce Lee and I used to fantasize about fighting; I used to dream that if I could just learn to defend myself like Bruce, my troubles would be over and no one would ever touch me again.

Beatings with a fishing rod would strip me of my dignity, and then he got more creative and stripped my clothes to beat me naked in front of the rest of the family. I lost dignity as well as hope that anyone would intervene.

Standing there, naked, being hit with that fiberglass fishing rod, I used to fantasize about using Karate to get out of the situation. In my fantasy, I would use the fiberglass fishing rod on him, to show him how it felt, and then I would break it so he would respect my knowledge to protect myself and he would never come near me again.

But that was only a fantasy in my head, so the beatings continued, my dignity dwindled, my fear grew and my story, that I meant nothing to no one, continued to be reinforced in my subconscious mind.

CHORES AND CHILD CARE

While our mother worked outside the home, it was up to me to take care of my siblings and get them off to school. Since they attended the grade school only a block away, we would all walk to school together. I would drop them off and continue walking another half mile to the junior high school.

MOVING TO GRAMMY'S!!!

This time we moved in with our grandmother, in the small two-bedroom house where my mother was raised.

The house was small so my siblings and I slept outside in a tent during the summer months and when winter arrived, we slept inside the house on the living room floor.

I was 12 years old, I loved my grandmother (we called her "Grammy"), our dad was rarely home so life seemed good. Our father seemed to be away a lot and in the mornings my mom would wake us up for school by playing music on the record player to get us up and moving for the day. We would listen to Bobby Sherman, The Partridge Family, Patsy Cline, Neil Diamond and Elvis. Life seemed to finally be calming down and the abuse from my father was practically non-existent due to the fact that Grammy was in the house.

One summer day, when my mom and Grammy were away at work, my father sent my sister and brothers outside to play, with strict instructions not to come back in the house until he gave them permission.

They knew better than to argue or request permission to go back in the house, even if they had to use the bathroom, so off they went to play in the yard.

I was told to stay in the house, work on my chores and my father told me he was going to go take a bath.

MORE SCARS

A little while later, my father called out to me and told me he wanted to see me. I walked into the bedroom and found him sitting on the bed, naked. He told me to sit on the bed beside him. As he started talking to me, his breathing changed, and then he pushed me back on the bed and took my clothes off of me. His breathing was heavy and he told me that he needed to teach me something very important. He told me that if any boy or man tried to touch me the way he was touching me that it was wrong and that I should not allow it.

The events that took place after he removed my clothes will be forever seared into my memory from the beginning of the attack until the end, when I had to clean the bedspread to get rid of any evidence of what had taken place.

Afterward, I was so confused, scared, repulsed, and afraid. He kept telling me over and over that I could not tell anyone what had happened. He told me that if I ever told anyone, he would get into a lot of trouble. I could sense that his fear of getting into trouble made him angry and his anger was something I wanted to avoid at all cost.

I soon realized that there was no help for what had just happened, but my bigger concern was finding a way to keep it from happening again.

DAD LEAVES THE FAMILY

Several months later we moved into our own home and soon after my father left my mother and ran off with his "lady friend". I came home from school one day to find my mother's wedding dress, pictures, and other memories in the trash can. My mother had tried to do everything my father demanded, but in the end, he left her anyway, with five children and no financial support.

FROM THE FRYING PAN TO THE FIRE

My father was gone, but life seemed to take a turn for the worse. At that point, my mother went after me with everything she had. She would constantly scream at me and tell me that "I looked just like my father, I acted just like my father and the sight of me made her sick!" She worked; I went to school, came home, cooked, cleaned, did the laundry, ironed, cared for my siblings and assumed the role of mother and homemaker. I was 14 years old.

If my mother would come home from work to find me napping on the couch, she would pull me by the hair until I fell off the couch and scream at me for not completing my chores. There was little time to think about homework and no time to be a kid.

THE OTHER MAN

During my sophomore year, while still married to her second husband, my mother changed jobs and met a man she would have an on-again off-again affair with for the next 36 years.

While she was sneaking off to their private rendezvous I was left to tend to my siblings, household chores and my stepfather.

PLANNING MY FUTURE

Many people assumed I got married at a young age because I wanted to get out of the house. Actually, I was married at age 17 simply because that seemed like the next logical step for me. I had been taking care of my siblings, cooking, cleaning, doing laundry, ironing and being the main caregiver in our home. I had been taking care of people since I was six years old; there was no opportunity to have a childhood or learn who I was, what I wanted to become or who I wanted to be with. I only had two requirements for my husband, "that he didn't hit me and didn't have affairs.

When a child is told something often enough, soon he or she believes it to be true. I was told that I was worthless, that I would never amount to anything, that I was trash, and, more often than I can count; my mother used to scream at me that she should have thrown me away and kept the afterbirth.

The spiritual meaning of every situation is not what happens to us, but what we do with what happens to us and who we decide to become because of what happens to us.

The only real failure is the failure to grow from what we go through.

- Marianne Williamson

MY CONFESSION

It wasn't until after I got married that I finally worked up the courage to tell my husband that my father had molested me. Once I spoke the words out loud and the earth did not open up and swallow me and God did not strike me dead, I felt liberated. I found that I could talk about it without feeling like I had done something wrong and I started to feel less self-loathing. When I finally worked up the courage to tell my mother, she just stood there and said, "I knew it. That son of a bitch, I knew it." I stared at her and then asked her, "If you knew what he was doing to me, why didn't you help me?" She just looked at me with fire in her eyes and said, "What was I going to do? I had five kids. If I tried to go against him; he would have left me alone with you five kids."

Feeling abandoned once again, I replied, "He left you anyway, you should have helped me." Then my mother looked at me and said "you have no idea what I have gone through to raise you five kids" and at that moment, I knew I was still on my own.

I often wondered what it would be like to have a mother who baked, loved and nurtured me and I vowed I would be the mother that I never had when I had children of my own.

THE BEGINNING OF THE END

As much as I wanted to believe that my marriage had turned out better than my parents' marriage, the truth was, I had once again learned to keep secrets in my home. My marriage was built on lies and "things we didn't talk about" and one day it all came to a head.

Our discussion started like so many times before. He was angry and I knew from his body language that he didn't want to talk about it. He never wanted to talk; he always just wanted the incident to go away.

As I started talking, he was sitting on the edge of the bed, his back to me and the more I tried to talk to him the more agitated his body language became. Then he started pounding his fists on either side of him, as though the mattress was a drum, and he continued pounding on the mattress.

Immediately I sensed that this was a situation far worse than I had ever dealt with before in our married life.

I felt the urgency to diffuse the situation so I decided to get up and walk away for a while to give him a chance to calm down until we could talk. As soon as I walked in front of him he stood up, grabbed me by the shoulders and physically threw me into a set of mirrored closet doors. I hit the doors with such force I do not know how they didn't shatter into a million pieces. As the back of my head hit the mirrors my immediate thought was "this can't be happening, he can't mean this, there must be some mistake, and even, how can I help him?"

But when I landed on my feet and stood facing him, I saw fire in his eyes and spit coming out of his mouth. The realization hit hard that I had not found a husband who would never hit me.

"Men feel threatened by women; because they are afraid women will laugh at them." "Women feel threatened by men because they're afraid of being killed." - Gavin De Becker

MIS-TAKE

I teach my clients that a mistake is a great opportunity to learn a better way. In the movies, when they are shooting a scene they may have to film it numerous times before they get it right. I am sure you are familiar with the movie term, "Action, take one." Then they shoot it again and say "Action, take two." I like to call this a mis-take.

This gives the word "mis-take" a positive spin because it allows you the opportunity for a re-take, over and over until you get it the way you want it! It's just like taking a picture, if you aren't happy with the results, you can take it again until you get the look you want!

A belief is a thought, fueled by a feeling that you think over and over again until it becomes habitual. Once a thought becomes habitual, you no longer even recognize that you are thinking it. For this reason, it is absolutely essential to identify and release the long held, worn out beliefs that often hold toxic thoughts in place. ~ Iyanla Vanzart

Chapter 3

MY MOTHER RETURNS

Something amazing happened when I filed for divorce; my mother came into my life. Since my mother had been absent most of my life, I was a little surprised to get a call from her one day. She asked "is there something I should know?" I really didn't see why I should have to go into the mess I was going through regarding my divorce, but I also had no reason not to answer her question. So I told her the truth; "I had filed for divorce." She then asked me what had happened and I gave her a brief summary. "Nancy," she said, "I have not been there for you your whole life. All of your life you have had to take care of everyone else. Please give me the chance to be there for you now while you are going through this."

WOW, who was this woman and what had she done with my mother? I was speechless and didn't know what to say. Having never had her in my life meant that I didn't even know where to start to let her help me.

So we just took it one day at a time. Every day we would talk on the phone and she would ask me how I was doing. She would always tell me that she loved me and that she was there for me. She even bought a cell phone and learned how to text so she could stay in touch and send me messages throughout the day letting me know she was thinking of me and that she was behind me 100%!

During this process my mother and the man she had been seeing for the past 36 years got married to each other. I can't begin to understand her 36 year journey with this man and the choices they made to be together while each of them were married to someone else. I do know that her choices have given her insight to be there for me when I seemed to have needed her the most. And for that I am grateful. We have many years to make up for and have begun working together to support each other.

Recently my mother asked me a question. "Nancy, how can I make it up to you? How can I go back and undo what I have done?"

My answer was, "Ma, you can't undo the past. All we can do is leave the past in the past, learn from our mis-takes, honor each other in the present and we will build a better 'us' in the future!"

Chapter 4

MY MOTHER'S STORY
(As told to me by my mother)

Nancy and I never had the opportunity to create a mother/daughter bond; not that I didn't want to, my heart yearned for that very thing from the moment she was born.

In 1956, at the age of 18, I had just graduated from high school, got married, moved to California and discovered I was pregnant; all within 5 months.

On my wedding day, I felt like Cinderella at the ball; complete with white gown and guests to wish us well. My mother made sure our wedding reception would be a day for me to remember and we celebrated right there on the farm with friends and family. As we celebrated our wedding day, I couldn't help but look around that farm with mixed emotions.

As I looked around, my thoughts drifted to my parents; my father came to the United States from Italy; he met my mother, they married, moved to our 40-acre farm in Ohio, and settled down to work the farm while raising eight children. Being a strict disciplinarian, my father kept me and my seven siblings close to home.

We were raised to work on our farm and he felt that school was less important than working in our fields. School activities and friends were not part of our lives; when school was in session, we woke up, completed our morning chores, walked the half mile trek down our lane to catch the bus, came home and worked on the farm until the sun went down.

My father ruled the house with an iron fist and a closed mind; communication was unheard of in our family. My siblings and I did not talk with each other as he believed it slowed down our work; work that was necessary if we were going to have food when the weather turned cold.

In our family, sons and daughters worked side by side in the field, and were considered as valuable as any other tool on the farm.

Much like a prisoner walking away from prison and leaving the steel gates behind her, I was finally getting married, getting off of this farm, away from a home life that meant working like a field hand and off to the land of sunshine and movie stars. California, here I come!

The next day, with all of our belongings and wedding gifts packed into and on top of our car, we started for California and a life of wedded bliss. Or so I thought…

The farther we drove, my excitement mounted; I didn't want to miss any part of the trip as the farthest I had ever been from the farm was school and the occasional visit to relatives.

As the wheels turned, so did my mind and I felt myself falling into a reverie of how I met this man, my new husband, the person who rescued me from a life of toil and was now taking me to our new life...

… With the windows down and the wind blowing through my hair, my thoughts drifted off to how I met my husband… he was a friend of one of my brothers and we dated. Actually, you can't really call it dating because we never really went out on dates; my father would have never allowed that.

At school, his sister and I shared the same classes and fell into an easy friendship. There was never an opportunity to visit with my friend outside of school because she lived in town and I lived on the farm. During the summer between my junior and senior year of high school, my brothers had access to a car and because my father worked an afternoon shift at the factory, my brothers would take me into town to visit my friend.

While my father was at work, we would sneak off of the farm to explore life "in town." Because my father did not mind me earning money, I was able to baby sit and clean house for our neighbor.

I would save my money; looking forward to my next visit to town to buy movie magazines and see the latest Hollywood Musical. Movies like Showboat, Singing in the Rain, and On Moonlight Bay, my heroes were Ava Gardner, Debbie Reynolds, and Doris Day!

My outings in town and to my friend's house were short lived because during this time, her family moved to California. For the rest of the summer, I spent my summer days on the farm wishing I had somewhere to go. Imagine my excitement when, six weeks later, her family moved back. I was happy to have my friend back and she encouraged my visits and my friendship with her brother.

Shortly after they returned from California, my future husband enlisted in the Army. I lost touch with him until my sister began writing him and suggested he write me. In the 1950's this was definitely considered dating!

After being discharged from the Army, he settled near my home town in Ohio, lived with his aunt and uncle, and found a job with a good future. I graduated in May of 1956, found a great job and worked until we married in September.

As we drove along the famous Route 66, I was pulled from my reverie when my husband started talking in an excited tone, telling me he could hardly wait until we reached Norman, Oklahoma. Wondering what was waiting for us in Norman Oklahoma, I tried to match his excitement and asked him what we were going to do there.

He laughed and told me that one of his army buddies lived there on a sheep farm and he wanted to make a surprise visit. He then went on to tell me that while they were serving together, his buddy told him stories about some of the men who work on their sheep farm and how these men have intercourse with sheep because sheep are considered the closest thing to a woman.

I looked at my new husband in horror as he went on to explain why he wanted that experience. The closer we got to Norman Oklahoma, it was apparent that he could hardly think of anything else.

As soon as the words were out of his mouth, watching his mounting excitement as he drove, I felt a fear like I had never known begin to take hold of my body. I stared out the window and wondered; "while he is having sex with sheep, what will I be doing?"

The farther we drove, the more he started sharing about his escapades during his army days along the Arizona border. Prostitutes, sex and the things he had done with other women started to make my head swim. This was unlike anything I had ever seen in the musicals I loved so much; not what I thought a honeymoon was supposed to be. Who was this person I was married to?

My mind began to spiral into an abyss that would all too soon become my reality.

The farther we drove, the more he talked and every instinct inside me told me that this marriage was a mistake. Panic began to overtake me as I wondered; "what am I going to do?" What could I do? I couldn't go back home, my father didn't even want me to marry this man, and something told me he would never be open to my return. I knew that I had to keep moving forward; turning back was not an option.

As we traveled west, we kept seeing large billboards advertising "Winslow For Men". That was when my husband remembered something that he had heard, "Winslow Arizona was known for having 3 women for every man." Suddenly he gave up the idea of stopping in Oklahoma because the opportunity to be with 3 women at one time appealed to him even more. I felt like I had just dodged a bullet, only to have more bullets zinging past my head.

Again I kept thinking, "What is he going to do with me while he's entertaining himself?" Once we reached Winslow, Arizona, he discovered that the advertisement was describing a department store for men and their tagline was describing 3 sales clerks to wait on each male customer. As I watched my new husband morph from a heightened state of arousal to one of anger, I began to see the pattern that was about to become my new life.

I can still remember the smell of California, as we stepped out of the car to greet his parents; the palm trees, the balmy weather and my unwavering hope that our discussions during the drive were over.

We slept in his parent's bed that evening and, during sex, the bed broke. I was humiliated, embarrassed and mortified. Sex with my husband was never the tender experience I thought it would be, nor was there any romance like my favorite Doris Day movie; there was no tenderness, romance or intimacy. Sex was always brutal and forced; never tender and loving, and not at all like I thought "love" would be. It took me years to understand that this was not love, but, at the time it was all I knew.

While my husband and his father were making a big issue of the bed being broken and laughing about it, I kept thinking, "What kind of stupid and horrible people am I married to? Something told me to keep my mouth shut and not to voice my opinion. I never,

ever, voiced my opinion while I lived at home and I wasn't about to start now! At least the farm was familiar territory to me and I could find solace in my work. Here, I knew no one. I was in a strange place, far from my mother, my family and any security I had ever known.

My husband found a job and we finally moved into an apartment in Long Beach, California. We were three blocks from the ocean and I could hear the ship's fog horns in the night. I loved hearing those sounds and I loved walking to the beach. The sound of the fog horns reminded me of far off places; places I would like to be or maybe escape to. While he was away at work, I walked to the beach every chance I got; I would sit for hours looking out over the Pacific Ocean.

In October I got very sick; every day I felt as though I were near death from being so sick; I felt alone, scared and thought I was dying.

This was yet another reminder of just how naïve I was; when I learned that my sickness was due to being pregnant.

For the first three months of my pregnancy I was so sick I could hardly hold my head up. One day my mother-in-law stopped by, only to tell me that I was being ridiculous and that I should get up and take care of my husband. During my pregnancy we moved back to his parent's home and I no longer had the opportunity to spend my days at the beach. The days were long, the nights were longer and towards the end of my pregnancy we moved to our own apartment.

It was here that I met the most wonderful friend; her name was Annie. When I went into labor, my husband took me to the hospital. I had no idea what to expect and was so excited when my husband brought Annie to visit that I actually began to feel hope.

Annie didn't return to the hospital during the rest of my labor and soon, the labor intensified and I became a new mother to a beautiful baby girl. I was scared, my mother was thousands of miles away, I had no one to turn to, and didn't know what to expect.

I laid in my hospital bed, wondering why Annie stopped coming by to see me only to have Annie call me to tell me that she wanted nothing more to do with me. I knew that my husband had also gone after her. Having just lost my only real friend, I felt a tremendous sadness. Unfortunately, Annie was the first of many of my friends that my husband would make sexual advances towards. This became a pattern with all of my women friends, and soon, I stopped trying to make friends.

After returning home from the hospital, I was not allowed to pick up my child or hold her and just love her.   When I brought her home from the hospital I had visions of holding and rocking my first child but I was not allowed.

My husband was adamant about the fact that she had to either be in bed or in the playpen.

She was a very good baby, but when she was in bed or in the playpen sometimes she would cry and some maternal instinct told me that she wanted to be held but I was not allowed to hold her. When I tried to talk him into letting me hold her, he become abusive if I insisted.

I learned to stop asking, just let it go, and did what he told me to do. Because I was forced to leave her in her crib, I was only allowed to hold her long enough to feed her and diaper her. So many mixed feeling were going through me but I learned to keep them all to myself.

There were always horrible, filthy books in our home. Books that I didn't know existed, books that depicted sex in ways I would not thought possible between two or more people.

We couldn't afford a television but he rented Super 8 movies and forced me watch them with him. Movies that showed sexual acts with women, dogs, and horses, to the point where I learned to finally tune them out and see nothing except my beautiful sleeping child in the crib next to us.

I never knew a life like ours existed and now I was living it every day. How could I tell anyone without being persecuted or judged?

Soon after my return from the hospital, he told me he wanted to have sex while I was still bleeding because it excited him. He told me if I didn't give in to him he would go out and buy sex. I should have told him to "drop dead", but I was scared, sick at heart, and disappointed in the way my life had turned out.

Within months, I began to feel that familiar feeling of movement and I knew that once again, I had another life growing inside of me.

I went to the doctor to confirm my thoughts and 10 months after the birth of my first child, I gave birth to another daughter. Thankfully, during my second pregnancy I was lucky not to have morning sickness. I played with and loved my first child while my husband was at work and awaited the birth of my second child.

Shortly after our second child was born, once again, we moved. One day, as I was out walking, checking out our new neighborhood with my daughters, I saw a woman throw a baby stroller in the trash. I waited until she was out of sight, pulled the stroller out of the trash and put my baby inside for the rest of the walk home.

A few months after our second child was born my husband told me he was tired of living in California and wanted to move to back to Ohio.

The thought of being near my family was twofold; I was looking forward to seeing them and at the same time, wondering how I would keep the true nature of our marriage from them.

Once again, with our few belongings packed inside and on top of the car, pulling a trailer behind us, we began our trip to Ohio. We got as far as the top of the San Bernardino Mountains; it was so foggy that we could hardly see the hood ornament on the front of our car. As I tried to keep the children quiet during that treacherous route, I felt that it was only by the grace of God that we were able to get through the fog.

No sooner had we gotten past the fog, our car broke down. My husband called his father, and we waited, there on the side of the rode, for his father to arrive and tow our car back to their home. Thankfully, my husband was determined to get back to Ohio. My oldest sister sent enough money for me and my two girls to fly home.

My relief at being away from my husband was short lived as he soon had our car repaired and joined us in Ohio.

We lived with my sister and her husband until my husband found a job; it was important to him that we find our own place as soon as possible so we could be alone to explore his sexual appetites. He found us a place that served as Army housing during the war until he decided to buy us a house. I noticed that my family started to grow distant from me. They had no idea what was happening in our home, but looking back they must have sensed that something was not right. How do you ask for help when you can't speak about what is going on? I watched my family grow more distant and my life became more isolated.

We moved into our house in May of 1960, in August our first son was born, in December of 1961 our second son was born and in June of 1963, our third son was born.

While I stayed home, cooking, cleaning, looking after our 5 children and servicing his needs, he worked and frequented the bar scenes. I began ironing other people's clothes to make up for the money he was spending at the bars. I was so excited when I was able to save up somewhere in the amount of $150.00 because I wanted to buy a sewing machine. I made the mistake of telling my husband how much I had saved; he took the money and bought a hunting rifle.

One of the windows in our home faced a window to the guest bedroom in our neighbor's home. Our neighbor had a sister who frequently stayed in their guest room. You could see right into their bathroom from the second floor of our home. My husband spied on her constantly to get aroused and when I sensed what he was doing, I made sure to keep the children near me so they would not accidently stumble upon him. When I argued with him about it, it only made our life worse.

In the fall of 1963 my husband decided he was tired of Ohio and told me to prepare to move back to California. Since we now owned our home and had purchased it through an Army loan, I figured we would have a little time until the house sold. When I asked him about selling the house, he informed me that he had no intention of selling the house and if the Army wanted it, they could have it after we left. I hated to leave my home and my family, but what was the use... I couldn't tell anyone what our life was like so I resigned myself to move, once again.

He and my brothers built a trailer and in November of 1963, we packed all we could in the trailer and drove back to California. We stayed with his parents again; there were thirteen of us in a three bedroom, one bathroom house.

A month later, we found a realtor who was selling homes for a hobby. She wanted to win a contest of "having sold the most homes for the month" and agreed to loan us the money to buy a home.

She arranged for us to buy the house, she won the contest, but she didn't get her money back that she loaned us. I don't remember how we got out of that arrangement but we only lived there for three years and in June of 1965 he decided he wanted to move back to Ohio. My brother and sister-in-law drove out, helped us pack up our truck with attached camper and their car. There was little room for our belongings and many things were left behind. Once again, we were on that all too familiar journey to Ohio.

We found a house to rent, he found a job at the food warehouse where he worked prior to our move to California; I finally worked up the nerve to tell him I would never move across country again and that we would have to stay settled in Ohio.

He changed jobs like we changed addresses; we stopped being practicing Catholics and he decided we should become practicing Nazarenes.

We went to church quite often, but because we moved so much we never quite got established until he finally settled on a Nazarene church just a few miles from where we were living. He became a pillar of the church and volunteered with the youth group. This meant that there were plenty of young women for him to prey upon. I constantly lived in fear of someone finding out about his true nature and when women turned their back on me in church, I knew that he had once again shown his true colors.

I found a job cleaning offices in the evening and took my children to work with me. It was hard to hide the money I earned and whenever he would come across some of the money I was saving, he would buy camping equipment. This meant there was usually no money for groceries, utilities or rent.

When I could, I would pay the utilities and rent and we usually relied on the church members to bring us food. My mother would buy school clothes for the children, but more often than not, we went without.

My husband told me about a friend of his who was having problems with her husband and she became a constant visitor in our home. One night he told me he was going out with her. I remember staying up all night, sitting out on the patio, and waiting up for him to come home. Try as I might, I could not find a way out of this life.

Sometimes, life can take an unexpected turn that will alter your future. My husband's grandmother died and his grandfather was now alone in his 3 story house. My husband talked his grandfather into letting us move in with him; we moved again, the children changed schools again and life got worse.

It was terrible living there, the generation gap was too large, I couldn't keep the children quiet enough and my husband was never home. Lucky for me, his grandfather lived across the street from a large hospital. One day I told the children, "I'm going to go to the hospital, get a job there, and get us away from this house."

In the meantime my father died and my husband saw an opportunity to have someone else care of us. In an effort to get the children out of that environment, I asked my mother if we could stay with her. We left his grandfather's and moved in with my mother, forcing the children to change schools once again

As there were only two bedrooms in my mother's home, the children stayed outside in a pop-up trailer and my husband and I stayed in the second bedroom. I continued to work at the hospital, my mother worked and my oldest daughter became the children's caregiver.

My husband worked night shifts and would sometimes be home with the children during the day.

One day I saw an advertisement for new homes not far from my mother's house. They were advertising that in lieu of a down payment, homeowners would have the option to paint the inside of the house and put in their own yard, thus fulfilling the down payment requirements to become homeowners.

We took them up on the offer, moved into our new home, changed schools again, began to get established in our new home and within months, my husband left town for Georgia, with his boss' secretary. They were gone for six weeks, when they returned, she went back to her husband and he wanted a divorce.

I thought I would die and I felt as though I truly wanted to die. I was scared and had no idea how I was going to raise my children.

When I asked him how I would raise our children without him, he told me to let my mother and my brothers take care of us and that I should not to even think about alimony or child support because he was moving back to California and I couldn't get blood out of a turnip.

My brothers did help me put in the yard, the children and I managed but I had not learned from my past. During the sixteen years I was married to my children's father, I had never learned who I was.

Looking back, I know I wasn't the best mother and yet, I try to remember the positive that I tried to bring into their lives; we listened to records, watched old movies, read, and sang. I was angry at being left alone to raise five children, angry that my husband had left me, dealing with the guilt of being glad my husband was out of my life and yet, I was unable to understand who I was and had no idea that I was forcing my children to deal with my anger and abuse.

When I was still married to their father, I thought that if I kept them quiet and took my anger and frustration out on my children that it would be easier on them than if their father took his anger and abuse out on them.

What I really taught them was "me". I showed anger and frustration in my body language, in my voice, and through my own attempt to find happiness in my life and I hurt my children in many ways. For this, I am so sorry and nothing I ever do will allow me to go back and undo the damage and the hurt I caused them while I felt trapped in the life we were living.

I lost my children while trying to find myself. I continued to make mistakes, I continued to be angry and I continued to hold on to my guilt. My guilt was all consuming and it blinded me to opportunities to create new relationships with my children.
And then, 38 years later, something happened that started a series of events leading me back to my oldest daughter.

When I found out that she was going through a divorce, I contacted her and asked her to please let me be there for her because I knew that divorce could be a devastating experience.

How could I have ever known that despite the darkness that robbed her of her childhood, she would become a beacon of light that others would be drawn to for strength and guidance? How could I possibly have known that she would be my salvation? What I was unable to teach her, she is now teaching me and her voice is strong with a message of hope for anyone who has heard or read her words. She teaches women that they can "do" or "be" anything they want, regardless of where they come from.

She is absolutely correct, and if I can do it, so can you.

Instead of giving up on herself the way I gave up on her, she kept going. I would not be sharing my story with you today if she were not the powerful woman she is. She chose to share her story with the world, in the hope that she can show all women the inner strength that they possess.

Thank you Nancy Mueller, for never giving up on yourself even when I told you that you would never amount to anything. I am proud of you, not just because you are my daughter, but because you have given me the courage to share my story! Your book and the love you showed while teaching me to look inside myself have helped me to eliminate and heal my guilt. – Josephine Mueller Christensen

Chapter 5

Perception Is Everything

You have just read two stories; mine and my mother's. After reading my story, I am sure you had many questions about the parenting choices my mother made.

After reading my mother's story, were you able to see my mother's parenting choices in a different light? We shared our stories to help people understand that unless you are able to come to terms with your own life's journey, you will take your beliefs, fears, limiting behaviors and even your dreams (or lack of) for the future and instill them in your children.

For years I believed that I was worthless, that I would never amount to anything, that I was unworthy of love and that I was on my own in this life. It took me years of working with therapists, coaches, spiritual teachers, and my own willingness to understand my limiting beliefs to realize that what I believed to be true about myself, "My Story" was really a continuation of my mother's story.

I believe I was born with a gift to keep searching for my true self and once I discovered "ME" and began to live an empowered life, it became part of my mission to teach other women how to find their true self.

This book is a journey to our New Beginnings, how we chose to break the cycle of our limiting beliefs and how we did it. My wish is that something I have written will give you the strength to keep moving forward and empower you to believe that you can do, be, or have anything you want, regardless of where you come from.

Because my childhood was full of fear and self-loathing, it took many years for me to realize that I had been given a gift to experience certain challenges in my life, the Inner Strength to persevere and the opportunity to teach others how they can move past their limiting beliefs.

Always remember: Perception is everything.

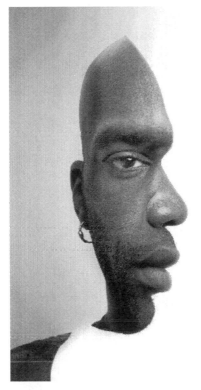

What we perceive to be true or a real memory may not be accurate.

Much like this picture, we often see things only one way. There are many ways to view experiences and the world around us.

I am honored for this opportunity to share my story with you in the hope that you will look beyond the person, embrace the optimism, and believe that your past is not who you are. You can change your past by changing your choices in the present. Live in the present, live in "the now" because Life Is All About Choices! When we can see someone for who they are and not where they came from we honor their presence.

Our Deepest Fear

Our deepest fear is not that we are inadequate. Our deepest fear is that we are powerful beyond measure. It is our light, not our darkness that most frightens us.

We ask ourselves "who am I to be brilliant, gorgeous, talented, fabulous?"

Actually, who are you not to be?
You are a child of God.

Your playing small does not serve the world. There is nothing enlightened about shrinking so that other people will not feel insecure around you. We are all meant to shine, as children do. We were born to make manifest the glory of God that is within us. It is not just in some of us, it is in everyone. And as we let our own light shine, we unconsciously give others permission to do the same.
As we are liberated from our own fear, our presence liberates others. ~ Marianne Williamson

Chapter 6

Shift Happens

At the time of this writing, I am 57 years old and my mother is 76. We talk, Skype or text every single day to stay in touch with each other, support each other, encourage each other and laugh.

We hold no anger, animosity, guilt or shame; we simply love and appreciate each other for who we are. After my first book was published, it gave my mother the opportunity to open a door into her past that, until then, she had nailed shut. My book was very cathartic for her and it gave my mother the opportunity to give herself permission to examine the "story" she had been telling herself all of these years. My mother's love for me gave her the understanding that she was the creator of her story, thus, she had the power the change her story.

Once she started sharing her story, the healing began and she asked me to teach her the information I was teaching my clients and soon she was figuring out how she could apply what I was teaching her to her life.

SHIFT HAPPENS!

Whether you are:

- a daughter struggling to create a better relationship with her mother
- a mother struggling to create a better relationship with her daughter
- a wife looking for a better relationship with her spouse
- wanting to feel loved, heard and appreciated
- contemplating divorce
- in the middle of a divorce
- trying to put a divorce behind you
- dating and looking for a loving partner
- looking for financial success
- or wanting to improve your health, there must be a *SHIFT* in your thinking.

Every person has a story, some stories enrich our lives and some stories are full of limiting beliefs that hold us back from reaching our true potential. The second half of this book will show you how to "Change Your Story."

The "stories" we tell ourselves can become our limiting beliefs. One of my mother's limiting beliefs was that she could never tell anyone the true nature of her relationship with my father. She feared being judged by others and over the years, she allowed her fear to rule her choices. Fear is merely a surface emotion; when we feel fear, it is an opportunity for us to look deeper at the root cause of these fears.

Chapter 7

THE THEORY OF THE MIND

Have you ever vowed to do things differently than the way your parents did things or that you were determined to change your life? The Theory of the Mind, by John G. Kappas gives us insight into how our stories are created.

When we are born, our mind is like a blank slate! The only part of our mind that we use is the Primitive Mind.

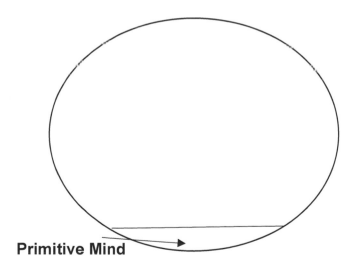

Primitive Mind

We fear only 2 things:

1. Falling
2. Loud Noises

All other fears, beliefs, and known associations are learned through environment, peers, and our caregivers (parents, teachers, grandparents etc.).

Between the ages of birth to 8 – 15 years of age, we create "known associations" in our subconscious mind. These "known associations" are thoughts, beliefs, (our story) that we believe to be absolutely true.

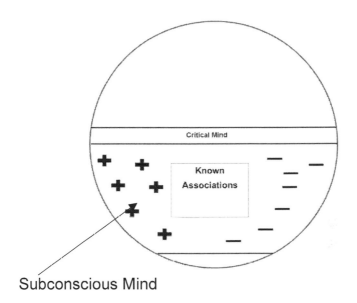

Subconscious Mind

Known Associations:

Positive vs. Negative | You are smart | You are stupid

Money comes easily | Money is only for the rich | The stove is hot

Candy is good | Work hard and save your money

etc.

Once the critical mind has been formed, we begin to question what we believe to be true or what we have been told (think about the teenage years).

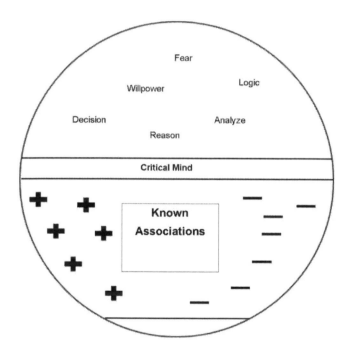

Conscious Mind = 12%

Subconscious Mind = 88%

When you understand that your **Known Associations** become your beliefs, your beliefs become your thoughts, your thoughts become your words, your words become your story, your story affects your choices AND all of this is being done on a subconscious level – you will then understand the importance of eliminating your limiting beliefs.

What is a Limiting Belief?

A limiting belief is merely the negative conditioning you may have grown up with. If you are going to be successful in creating the life of your dreams, you have to believe that you are capable of making it happen. You have to believe you have the right stuff and that you are able to pull it off. You have to believe in yourself.

➢ Knowing that the Conscious portion of your mind is working at 12% capacity, you can see that attempting to make the changes you want to happen in the conscious mind alone are not enough

➢ Your Conscious mind will bring your issues into your awareness

➢ Your Conscious mind works during your waking hours

➢ Your Subconscious mind is working at 88% capacity and is working 24/7

➢ If your Subconscious mind is working 24/7 and thinking thoughts you are not even aware of, how do you bring these thoughts to the surface?

If your purpose for reading this book is because you are hoping to heal a relationship, it is important to understand that not all people will find it necessary to share their story with each other to make changes in their relationship.

But it does help to understand that there may be things about each of you that the other has no way of knowing.

It is up to each of us to heal ourselves and take 100% responsibility for our actions.

Chapter 8

YOU Create Your Reality

How many of you know someone who is always late, and when they finally show up, they always have a plethora of excuses? Did you ever hear someone show up late to an event and tell you they were late because of traffic? Wouldn't it be refreshing to have someone just be honest and say, "I am late because I left the house late!"?

In his book, The Success Principles, Jack Canfield shares how his mentor, W. Clement Stone taught Jack to take 100% responsibility for his life. Taking 100% responsibility means you acknowledge that you create everything that happens to you. It means you understand that you are the cause of all of your experiences.

We must all learn that we are responsible for the choices we make in our lives and that we must give up blaming someone or something else for where we are.

- ➤ You choose to eat the junk food
- ➤ You choose not to exercise your mind and body
- ➤ You choose to stay in a job you hate
- ➤ You choose to stay in your comfort zone rather than try new opportunities
- ➤ You choose to go against your better judgment
- ➤ You choose to give up on your dreams
- ➤ You choose not to deal with your relationships
- ➤ You choose to hold on to your negative past
- ➤ You choose to do everything yourself instead of asking for help

THE GOOD NEWS IS...

Every negative has a positive...

- ➤ You CAN learn to eat healthier
- ➤ You CAN learn to say "no" to peer pressure
- ➤ You CAN find a better job
- ➤ You CAN say "yes" to great opportunities

➢   You CAN earn a living when you are living your life on purpose

➢   You CAN hire that coach, teacher or mentor

➢   You CAN listen to your "inner voice"

➢   You CAN find the exercise program that is "right" for you

When you take full responsibility and accept that you are making the **CHOICE** to move forward (or stay where you are), the next step is to stop complaining ... or... take the risk of not being able to create your life exactly the way you want it.

Chapter 9

Changing Your Story

Ok, so you may be asking yourself "How Can I Change My Story?

I am so glad you asked that question!

The answer is simple – it's all about what you BELIEVE to be true.

That being said, I want you to know that there is a *HUGE* difference between what you BELIEVE TO BE TRUE (your story) and what is ACTUALLY TRUE (reality).

Here is an example: When you were little, you BELIEVED that Santa was real. You believed that to be true. As you got older and someone told you that Santa is part of the Christmas holiday, you were faced with changing your belief about Santa.

Every belief also has an emotion attached to it which creates a *feeling*. Let's take the example of Santa again. Depending on the presents Santa used to bring you (or didn't bring you) and then based on how someone broke the news to you about who Santa really is – has a huge impact on how you view Santa and the holiday gift giving scene in your adult life.

In his book, Karma Buster, Joe Nunziata teaches us that understanding how to deal with our feelings will move us in the direction of our heart's desires.

When was the last time you took the time to truly think about how you FEEL about situations and events that come up in your life? For many of us, we don't take the time to know what we are feeling because we are too busy "doing." We are always trying to set goals, accomplish our goals, trying to figure out "how" to get what we want, trying to figure out "what went wrong".

You can see that the list of why we don't take the time to know what we are feeling is endless.

Here's another example, let's say you were taught that it is the woman's duty to take care of the men. During family dinners, the men should always be fed first and once their needs were taken care of, it is then time for the women to eat. One day you have dinner at your friend's house and the women eat with the men, each person serves him and herself, everyone carried their dishes to the kitchen and both men and women helped clean up after dinner.

Now we are faced with the big question: "Who is right and who is wrong?"

The answer is: Neither belief is right nor wrong, your belief is your belief.

REMEMBER: Our subconscious mind makes up 88% of our mind and our conscious mind makes up the other 12%. When we are struggling with right or wrong, good or bad, we can only come to conclusions based on what we BELIEVE to be true, right, wrong, good or bad.

When you want to change your belief (your story) about serving dinner or your brand of coffee, changing your story may not seem very important, but what about when it comes to your health, your wealth, your relationships, your career or your goals?

Remember my mother's story? The one that she told herself, over and over about needing to be the wife my father wanted her to be so he would not leave her. How would her life have been different if she had given herself permission to pay attention to her feelings rather than her story that "this is the life she had been given and that she was helpless to do anything about it?"

In the 50's and 60's there was no one or no place for my mother to turn for advice. She was living a life of "hell on earth" and with no coaching, books, therapy or mentors to turn to, she believed that her path was set and there was no possible alternative to her plight.

Let's talk about health. A woman decides that she wants to lose 50 pounds. She goes on a diet, she goes to the gym, she does everything in her power to get control of her health and yet she struggles.

Rarely do people understand that the limiting beliefs, which are constantly streaming from our subconscious mind, has an effect on the outcome of our desires. Because losing 50 pounds also has a strong feeling attached to it (that she may not be consciously aware of) her subconscious mind *IS* aware of it and is keeping her from her desired outcome.

Our subconscious mind is working 24/7, whether we are awake, asleep, driving, working or playing.

Our conscious mind is only working while we are awake.

Remember: our Subconscious mind controls 88% of our mind and our Conscious mind controls 12% of our mind. So, if the Conscious mind wants to lose weight but the Subconscious mind has a "limiting belief" (your story) that is contrary to our desire – we have conflict between the conscious mind and the subconscious mind and the subconscious mind (88%) takes over.

Let's say that when this woman is taught to pay attention to her feelings about her weight loss, she realizes that she will look different and others will see her differently. She feels uncomfortable with the attention she may receive.

She realizes that men will look at her differently and now she fears what this kind of attention may bring based on her belief that women should "stay in the background". Can you see how her "story" is keeping her from her desired goal?

This is an example of weight, what about the limiting beliefs we have around success, money, family, parents, siblings, careers, relationships etc.?

How do we change these limiting beliefs so that we can create the life we want?

Understanding where these beliefs come from is the first step to eliminating them.

Every belief is based on something you were taught through "known associations". Known Associations are introduced to you from your parents, teachers, school, TV, Media, grandparents, culture, etc. from birth to 8 years of age.

Known Associations are things like:

- ➢ You are smart
- ➢ You are stupid
- ➢ You are pretty
- ➢ You are ugly
- ➢ You are fat
- ➢ Sugar is good
- ➢ Sweet is good
- ➢ The stove is hot
- ➢ Money is hard to come by
- ➢ Boys have more opportunities
- ➢ You come from a long line of big boned people
- ➢ There are 2 kinds of people: The "have's" & the "have not's"
- ➢ Don't speak to strangers
- ➢ Never argue with the IRS (Internal Revenue Service)
- ➢ Health (our family has always had health issues)
- ➢ Career (find a job, stick with it, move up the ladder, save money, retire)

- Self-Esteem
- Self-Worth
- Parenting
- Sex
- Your Mother
- Your Father
- Religion
- Being Gay
- Being Straight
- Your Home
- The Car You Drive
- Your bank account
- Marriage
- Death
- Divorce
- The Government
- The food you eat
- Respect your elders
- Adults have more rights than children
- Guilt
- Shame
- Daddy's little princess

If something in your life brings up feelings of negative emotions, this is an indication of something that you have not yet dealt with in your life and is guaranteed to keep you from your succeeding in areas of your life.

Chapter 10

My Limiting Belief

One of my limiting beliefs centered on my Self Worth. From the time I was a little girl, my mother used to tell me that I was worthless. She would say, "You're worthless, you're nothing and you will always be nothing. You are a "NOTHING BURGER (I had no idea what a Nothing Burger was but the way she used to say it to me told me that it was a really bad thing to be!) Needless to say, it didn't take long for me to realize and understand that I WAS "nothing" and would never amount to anything. I saw me and our family as the "have not's" and dreamed of being part of a family that looked like they "had it all!" So, when it came time to study in school, how much effort do you think I put into it? When a child is told something often enough, soon he or she will believe it to be true.

As an adult, I was perfectly capable of surviving in my life but it never occurred to me that I might be a success in my life. It wasn't until I was in my 30's with daughters of my own that I actually started rethinking my self-worth because I wanted to be the mother I never had.

Several years ago, my mother said to me, "Nancy, I had no idea you were so brilliant. When you were a little girl, you used to tell me about thoughts and ideas that you had and the things you came up with used to frighten me. I believed that the only way a woman could make it in this world was to be quiet and not bring attention to herself and you were always coming up with ideas that I thought were crazy. I used to scream at you and tell you to "shut up" and when screaming didn't work, I tried beating it out of you and when that didn't work, I just ignored you." Today I watch you teaching women and I often wonder what would have happened if I had listened to you when you were a little girl."

YOU SEE, MY LIMITING BELIEFS (MY STORY) WERE NOT EVEN MINE – THEY WERE MY MOTHER'S BELIEFS!!!

Feelings are our mind's way of telling us when something is or isn't right in our life. When I wanted to believe that I was a success, my limiting beliefs brought up all the old feelings of negative self-worth and it was a very difficult journey for me to travel because my conscious and my subconscious continued to do battle with everything I tried to learn.

The more successful I became, the more my limiting beliefs challenged those thoughts. The challenge is, too many people have lost the simple art of *FEELING* their feelings.

Remember, if every memory or belief has an emotion attached to it (and we know it does) it is important to understand the difference between an emotion and a feeling, so that we can get to the Belief, or Limiting Belief (our story) lurking in our subconscious mind.

Here are some emotions that indicate a feeling that needs to be dealt with:

> Anger
> Jealousy
> Anxiety
> Guilt
> Fear
> Sadness

When you're angry at something, this is a surface emotion letting you know that a belief that you believe to be true or untrue is being tested. Your job, is to figure out what that story is to keep it from continuously surfacing in your life.

Let's say that you have a fear of not having enough money. Money is a great example because people are always looking for ways to have more money in their life.

Our belief, or limiting belief(our story) instilled in us through known associations during our childhood is that we find a job that makes a lot of money and we don't change jobs unless we are forced to or find a job that pays even more money.

The problem with that is, what if you hate your job? Every Sunday at 4:00 you feel yourself getting depressed because you know that tomorrow morning you have to get up and go back to that place you hate and it ruins your night.

You look at Monday mornings as the worst time ever and you wish your life away eagerly awaiting Friday afternoon and the weekend to come.

Many people live their lives like this because of limiting beliefs. They don't believe that they could be doing something they love AND earn a living at it at the same time.

- ➢ They have FEAR around losing their job
- ➢ They have ANGER towards their co-workers
- ➢ They have GUILT about wanting something for themselves
- ➢ They are JEALOUS of people who seem to have jobs they love
- ➢ They are SAD that their life isn't turning out the way they had dreamed about

These emotions are letting you know that until you get to the real feelings and deal with them, you will continue to struggle.

Let's talk about GUILT

Guilt is a big one – especially for women because we are natural born nurturers and we are constantly trying to do things for other people.

We want time to our self, we want a different career, we want a better relationship with our parents or spouse but we are drowning in GUILT.

Guilt stems from a limiting belief linked to unresolved issues in our past.

Let's use the "losing weight" example again. A woman goes on a diet, she tries to eat healthier, and something comes up that causes her to choose to veer from her health goals.

The next day she is consumed with guilt because she veered from her health goals. Why is it so hard for her to simply give herself permission to make herself happy today and jump right back on her mission tomorrow?

Because Self-Love is very difficult for women. The thought of putting our needs first is very foreign to us. It FEELS wrong!

Think about someone you love very much.

Do you have that person in your mind?

Now, would you ever think of treating that person the exact same way you treat yourself?

If the answer is "NO" what are you prepared to do to start Loving Yourself as much as you love that other person?

I can promise you, if you are struggling with certain areas in your life, you are struggling because of your limiting beliefs. Our thoughts become our beliefs, our beliefs become our habits, and our habits become our choices. These choices then create a lifestyle that may leave you feeling a lack of energy, happiness or positive outlook on your current situation.

Chapter 11

The Missing Link

We have all heard about The Law of Attraction. What you think about, you bring about. One very important factor that people fail to mention when they talk about The Law of Attraction are the FEELINGS that go along with what you are wanting to attract. If you want a new car, more money, better relationships, a healthier body, etc. but you feel that you don't deserve them, it is impossible for the Universe to bring you what you desire because your feelings are energy and the Universal Law works on energy.

Now, with all of this information, how do you go about changing your life?

Let's take another look at those Known Associations:

- ➢ You are smart
- ➢ You are stupid
- ➢ You are pretty
- ➢ You are ugly
- ➢ You are fat
- ➢ Sugar is good
- ➢ Sweet is good
- ➢ The stove is hot
- ➢ Money is hard to come by
- ➢ Boys have more opportunities
- ➢ You come from a long line of big boned people
- ➢ There are 2 kinds of people: The "have's" & the "have not's"
- ➢ Don't speak to strangers
- ➢ IRS (Internal Revenue Service)
- ➢ Health
- ➢ Career
- ➢ Self-Esteem
- ➢ Self-Worth

- Parenting
- Sex
- Your Mother
- Your Father
- Religion
- Being Gay
- Being Straight
- Your Home
- The Car You Drive
- Your bank account
- Marriage
- Death
- Divorce
- The Government
- The food you eat
- Respect your elders
- Adults have more rights than children
- Guilt
- Shame
- Daddy's little princess

I WANT	WHAT WILL IT *FEEL* LIKE WHEN I HAVE IT?
To lose 30 lbs.	Happy – I will LOVE what I see in the mirror!
	Scared – I will receive more attention than I am used to receiving
To grow my business and make more money	Relieved – this will make me a successful woman
	Scared – others will see me as a success and I don't know if I can live up to that title. I may LOOK successful but I worry every day about making the right choices!

Make a list of your wants

> ➤ Look at the list and allow yourself to feel what it will FEEL like to obtain these things
>
> ➤ This is how you will know if you truly want them and what is holding you back

John Strelecky, author of The Why Café, Life Safari, The Big 5 For Life and Return to the Why Café teaches us that too many people get bogged down in life trying to figure out "how" to make their life better. John suggests that people begin to concentrate on their "Who's". Start asking yourself, "Who can I talk to, to get the answers I am looking for? Who can teach me the tools that would enrich my life? Who are the "Who's" in your life? Think about something that you wanted to accomplish and then think about when you accomplished it. Who were the people that came into your life to help you accomplish what you had set out to do?

Perhaps it was a person who introduced a new book to you. Perhaps it was a coach, mentor or teacher. Perhaps it was a character in a book or movie that gave you inspiration to take the next step to reach your goal. So often we tend to overlook the importance of the "Who's" in our life.

John also has a video on YouTube titled "Museum Day" – I recommend that each of you take 6 minutes out of your day to watch this video because it will change the way you think about how you are living your life.

Chapter 12

Limiting Beliefs

A limiting belief is merely the negative conditioning you may have grown up with. If you are going to be successful in creating better relationships and the life of your dreams, you have to believe that you are capable of making it happen. This is why it is so important that you understand "why" your story matters! You have to believe you have the right stuff and that you are able to pull it off. You have to believe in yourself.

So the next time you have a limiting belief that is holding you back, let's take this example and ask yourself this simple question:

5 things I want to change about my

_____ (health, self, wealth, career,

relationships, self-esteem, etc.):

1. _____

_____

2. _____

_____

3. _____

_____

4. _____

_____

5. _____

_____

Depending on the story you have told yourself to

this point in your life, this could be a very simple

exercise or an extremely challenging exercise! Feel

free to create this exercise for all areas of your life

_____ (health, self, wealth, career,

relationships, self-esteem, etc.).

On a separate sheet of paper or notebook, create categories: (Example: health, self, wealth, career, relationships, self-esteem, etc.). In each category, create a list of what you are currently doing that is not working for you and then come up with options to change those choices.

Chapter 13

Taking Action

Putting What You Have Learned Into Action (yes, YOU have to do the work)

What is holding you back?

1. _____

_____

_____

2. _____

_____

_____

3. _____

_____

_____

4. _____

_____

_____

5. _____

_____

What do you believe is causing you to feel this way?

_____

_____

_____

_____

_____

_____

_____

What are your limiting beliefs?

1. _____

_____

2. _____

_____

3. _____

_____

4. _____

_____

5. _____

_____

What do you believe is causing you to feel this way?

_____

_____

_____

_____

_____

_____

_____

What are your fears?

1. _____

_____

2. _____

_____

3. _____

_____

4. _____

_____

5. _____

_____

What do you believe is causing you to feel this way?

_____

_____

_____

_____

_____

_____

_____

What do you feel guilty about?

1. _____

   _____

2. _____

   _____

3. _____

   _____

4. _____

   _____

5. _____

   _____

What do you believe is causing you to feel this way?

_____

_____

_____

_____

_____

The answer to these questions can be found if you are willing to look in the mirror and be honest with yourself. Commit to 20 minutes every day to sit in a quiet place and ask yourself these questions. Think about events throughout the day that left you with negative feelings. Then think about "WHY" you felt that way. You must commit to opening your mind, being brutally honest with yourself and then understanding why you felt the way you did. This is your first step to understanding what you are thinking (believing your story) at the subconscious level.

Once you get in touch with what you are thinking, you can then determine if it is a "TRUTH" or what you "BELIEVE" to be the truth. When you know the difference, you are then able to start changing your story.

Chapter 14

What is Your Purpose

What Is Your Purpose for being on this earth? Whether you call it your Mission Statement or Your Life's Purpose, why do you think you are here?

If you do not know your purpose for being here, how do you know you are on the right path? How do you know if the choices you are making on a daily basis are in alignment with your higher self? Not knowing your purpose for being here is like getting in the car with no destination in mind. You will drive and drive but never know where you are going or if you have arrived!

Perhaps you are here to bring laughter to the world. You find that you enjoy making people laugh because you know laughter is good for the soul. Are you working in an industry that enables you to use your gift of laughter?

Maybe you love painting; are you making your living as a painter? Maybe you love to cook, are you making your living in the food industry? If you are working at a job you hate because you don't see a way to earn a living doing what you love, then find a "Who" who can show you how to live your purpose.

What are you passionate about? What do you love doing so much that you could spend hours doing it? Who do you know who is making a living doing what you love to do? What would it take for you to live your life, every single day, doing what you love?

What is your J.O.B. (Your **J**ump **O**utta **B**ed)? Remember the last time you woke up in the morning and remembered what day it was and the awesome activities you had planned for that day? Do you remember how you felt? I'll bet you wanted to **J**ump **O**utta **B**ed and get your day started. What would it take for you to feel that way every single day of your life?

In the space provided, list your idea of the perfect day:

_____

_____

_____

_____

_____

_____

_____

_____

_____

_____

_____

_____

_____

_____

_____

_____

_____

Chapter 15

The Perfect Day

Now, what would it take for you to be able to have that kind of day, every single day of your life?

_____

_____

_____

_____

_____

_____

_____

_____

_____

_____

_____

_____

_____

Chapter 16

I Want

Create a list of 5 "I WANT's:

What do you truly want in your life? More money, happiness, better health, a loving partner, a better career, children, etc. What do you truly want in your life? Start here and make a list (feel free to use a separate sheet of paper).

1. _____

   _____

2. _____

   _____

3. _____

   _____

4. _____

   _____

5. _____

   _____

If this is a list of what you truly want in your life, what is holding you back from having it?

Make a list of what is holding you back:

1. _____

   _____

2. _____

   _____

3. _____

   _____

4. _____

   _____

5. _____

   _____

Now take a look at your list of what is holding you back. Do you know that there is only one answer to this question? The only thing holding you back from having everything you want in this world is "YOU". Remember; "YOU" create your reality. This is often a difficult concept to accept because society is so used to blaming others for what they don't have.

When people don't have something they want, they will blame their parents, their education, the government, society, TV, their job, their boss, their co-workers, their spouse, etc. But the truth is, "YOU" are responsible for "YOU"!!! Please understand that EVERY TIME you blame someone or something else for your current circumstances, you are putting yourself in "Victim Mode".

This above all, refuse to be a victim.
- Margaret Atwood

When you think everything is someone else's fault, you will suffer a lot. When you realize that everything springs only from yourself, you will learn both peace and joy. ~ Dalai Lama

Don't Quit!

When things go wrong, as they sometimes will,
when the road you're trudging seems uphill,
When the funds are low and the debts are high,
And you want to smile, but you have to sigh,
When care is pressing you down a bit,
Rest, if you must, but do not quit.

Life is queer with its twists and turns,
As every one of us sometimes learns,
And many a failure turns about,
When he might have won had he stuck it out;
Don't give up though the pace seems slow
You may succeed with another blow.

Often the goal is nearer than,
It seems to a faint and faltering man,
Often the struggler has given up,
When he might have captured the victors cup,

And he learned too late when the night slipped
down,
How close he was to the golden crown.

Success is failure turned inside out
The silver tint of the clouds of doubt,
And you never can tell how close you are,
It may be near when it seems so far,
So stick to the fight when you're hardest hit
Its when things seem worst that you must not quit.

Anonymous

Chapter 17

Don't Quit Now

Now it is time to ask, "What is holding you back?"

F.E.A.R. = False **E**vidence **A**ppearing **R**eal

Create a list of 5 fears that have been holding you back and how these fears may still be holding you back.

1. _____

_____

2. _____

_____

3. _____

_____

4. _____

_____

5. _____

_____

When you are ready to make the commitment to change your story, you will also change your life.

Chapter 18

Creating Success

We are going to be replacing toxic thoughts (I can't) with positive thoughts "(success!!)

I am not a one in a million kind of girl.
I am a once in a lifetime kind of woman.

The easiest way to begin this program is to start with a brand new spiral bound notebook. As we move forward into the program, you may decide that you want to use something different, but for now, an inexpensive spiral bound notebook will work well.

Please remember, there is zero financial obligation to this exercise but you will be obligated to give your most valuable asset; **your time**. We can always make more money but time, once spent, can never be recovered. For this reason, this exercise is going to be your biggest investment yet!

Let's get started!

1. Habits and beliefs are something we create in our minds. Because our mind is so powerful, it is often difficult to eliminate limiting beliefs or habits. For this month, choose 2 habits that you currently have and agree to change them. This can be something very simple such as:
    a. Which hand you brush your teeth with
    b. The way you place a new roll of toilet paper on the holder
    c. Your routine in the shower (if you shampoo first, try doing that second) you get the picture, right?

These are small habits that cause no harm and yet each one is very powerful because it has become a part of you. This exercise is meant to show you how powerful our habits (subconscious) are. You will want to make notes in your notebook, on which habit(s) you decided to change and how difficult or easy they were to change.

2. Your "To Do" List! Do you have a "To Do" List? When you are able to cross something off of the list, do you see this as a success? Many women don't because they simply see these tasks as something to "get done."

List 5 things that you were able to cross off of your list. Write these down in your notebook. Beside each entry, write an explanation of "WHY" it needed to be done and how you completed it. Now, with these same 5 items, explain how completing these tasks made you *FEEL*.

Pictures!

We speak in words but we *THINK* in pictures. For this reason, we are going to find a picture to match each of your 5 successes.

For instance, if one of the tasks on your list was to order business cards, tape or glue one of your business cards in your notebook. Maybe one of your tasks was to put all of the holiday decorations away. Take a picture of the decorations in their storage area and place this picture in your notebook. Perhaps you FINALLY booked that dentist appointment!!!

Are you starting to see the value of this exercise?

These simple yet effective and powerful exercises will help you to start changing your habits, and recognizing successes.

Reminder: Procrastination never breeds success!

The information in this book has changed how I live my life and how I think about my life as well as changed the lives of many of my clients. I want to thank you for taking the time to read this book because I have seen these concepts and techniques in action.

The action portion of this book asks you to do a lot of feeling, thinking and getting in touch with your emotions. Meditating is the best way to "go within" to get in touch with your Higher Self to really understand your story and how to change it.

There are many methods of meditation and one that I have found to be extremely effective is The Golden Box Meditation. For more information on The Golden Box Meditation, please visit www.goldenboxmeditation.com.au

Epilogue

My mother grew up in a very sheltered environment knowing no other lifestyle except what she experienced growing up on her family farm. Knowing next to nothing about sex and the way the world worked, she chose to believe that her life had turned into a living nightmare.

She had no one to turn to and no resources at her disposal to try to find a way out of her situation. My father was and still is a sex addict. His choices and his addiction has adversely affected many people. Never let someone else's choices affect the life you could be living.

Addictions come in all forms. Many women find themselves unhappy, scared, desperate, depressed and even feeling hopeless. One popular addiction that may seem harmless is Retail Therapy. Take some time to look at your material possessions, those things you felt it was so necessary to buy. How do you feel now when you look at them?

Do they still bring you the wonderful feelings that you felt when you purchased them? Do they still bring you joy and happiness?

If not, why has that feeling left you? Were you simply shopping to fill a void? Retail Therapy can be an addiction just like any other addiction such as smoking, drinking, drugs, etc. Our addictions always SEEM like a great way to escape the real world but we all know that sooner or later, the real world takes over and we still have to deal with whatever we were trying to escape from.

Are you able to sit with your thoughts and meditate for at least 15 minutes? Are you able to go within your own mind to feel peace and acceptance? Or do you find it difficult to sit with your own thoughts because you are unhappy with where they lead you?

What do you feel is missing in your life? How can you fill this void? What would it take to make you feel truly happy and content?

Now that you know what is missing or lacking in your life, what are you prepared to do to get what you need and want?

Let's think about what you do on a daily basis to feed your soul? Your Soul is THE VERY ESSENCE OF WHO YOU ARE!! It is your life force. How are you nurturing your Soul on a daily basis? Just like any living thing, you must feed and care for it if it is going to grow.

Let's think of you as someone who is on this earth to fulfill a mission; Your Purpose. Now, let's think of "you" as someone who has two mindsets: your conscious mind and your subconscious mind. It is a known fact that our conscious mind works only while we are awake but our subconscious mind works 24/7. As previously mentioned, our subconscious mind rules 88% of our mind and our conscious mind only 12%. Stop to think about those odds for just a moment because your wants and desires come from your conscious mind but your beliefs come from your subconscious mind.

So, if there is any doubt or limiting belief somewhere in your subconscious mind that you can't have, don't deserve, aren't good enough or whatever else is lurking around in there, how do you EMPOWER your conscious mind and disempower your subconscious mind?

Ask yourself: What do I truly want? What would make me happy? Then, listen quietly to whatever comes to your mind, telling you that you can't' have it or why you can't have it.

These can be the first steps for you to understand the story you tell yourself about why you can't have what you want. Once you know your story, you will begin to understand your choices about what got you to where you are and what you need to change to get to where you want to be!

I hope this information has helped you to begin thinking in a different direction to have, do or be anything you desire in this lifetime.

Please understand that Empowerment starts from within. Empowerment is an INSIDE job and you are already a success in your life.

If you are wondering how you can get started realizing the success you have already brought into your life, how to keep being successful and how to keep moving towards your intended success to be the empowered woman you are, please feel free to connect with me, Nancy Mueller, at:

www.nancymuellerglobal.com or email me at info@nancymuellerglobal.com and if you are experiencing a life of depression, despair, hopelessness or addictions of any kind, please empower yourself by seeking help from a professional who is trained to guide you.

As I consistently used the tools and techniques listed in this book, I was able to emerge from the darkness in my life. One day during meditation, I wrote the following:

I lived in dark before I found the light,
I have always felt the need to fight

But now…
I have joy,
I have happiness, as my angels gather 'round

They are here to help me celebrate because I have cut the ties that had me bound!

I am love,
I am light,
I no longer feel the need to fight!

At this time, your story may be one of the Untold Stories, however, YOUR STORY MATTERS, and so do you. Please let my mother's story be the catalyst that will teach you to "never live a life of resignation".

Always Remember: **Life Is All About Choices**

Resources

1. Transitions by William Bridges
2. The Success Principles by Jack Canfield
3. Karma Buster by Joe Nunziata
4. My Story by Josephine Christensen
5. The Why Café by John Strelecky
6. Life Safari by John Strelecky
7. The Big 5 For Life by John Strelecky
8. The Mental Bank by John G Kappas
9. REMEMBER: Everything Is Possible by Michelle M Wright
10. Marianne Williamson
11. Iyanla Vanzart
12. Photos by Gayle Dawn Exton
13. Graphics by All We Print

TAKE AWAY

At the time of this writing, my oldest grandson is 16 years old. When he was 4 years old, we were preparing to have a family night of pizza and a movie at home.

While I was in the kitchen making the pizza dough, he walked into the kitchen, stood next to me, looked up at me and said, "Grammy, tonight we are going to **Party Like Purple!**"

He had such a huge grin on his face and I had no idea what he meant. And then I realized that he was looking forward to the evening with our family, feeling loved, secure and part of something bigger than himself. And the best way he could think to describe this feeling was "**Party Like Purple!**"

I think that **Party Like Purple** is a great way to sum up feeling loved, secure and knowing that you are part of something bigger than yourself.

It is my wish for you that you always **Party Like Purple** in your life!

Made in the USA
Lexington, KY
06 July 2016